# THE DANCES OF AFRICA

*To my wife Ghislaine Huet*
*for her invaluable collaboration in the discovery of Africa*

*Young Senufo girls dressed*
*for the* Ngoro *dance*

Translated from the French
*Danses d'Afrique*
by Dorothy Blair

Library of Congress Cataloging-in-Publication Data
Huet, Michel, 1917-
 [Danses d'Afrique (1994). English]
 The dances of Africa / [photos by] Michel Huet ; text by Claude
Savary ; [translated from the French Danses d'Afrique by Dorothy S.
Blair].
 p.  cm.
 Includes bibliographical references.
 ISBN 0-8109-3228-8
 1. Dance—Africa.  2. Africa—Social life and customs.
I. Savary, Claude, Ph. D.  II. Title.
GV1705.H8313  1995
793.3' 196—dc20                                          95-23201

English-language edition copyright © 1996 Thames and Hudson Ltd., London,
and Harry N. Abrams, Inc., New York
Photographs copyright © 1994 Michel Huet/Hoa-Qui
Text copyright © Claude Savary
Copyright © 1994 Éditions du Chêne—Hachette Livre

Published in 1996 by Harry N. Abrams, Incorporated, New York
A Times Mirror Company
No part of the contents of this book may be reproduced without the written
permission of the publisher

Printed and bound in Spain

# THE
# DANCES
## OF
# AFRICA

## MICHEL HUET

TEXT BY CLAUDE SAVARY

HARRY N. ABRAMS, INC., PUBLISHERS

# Contents

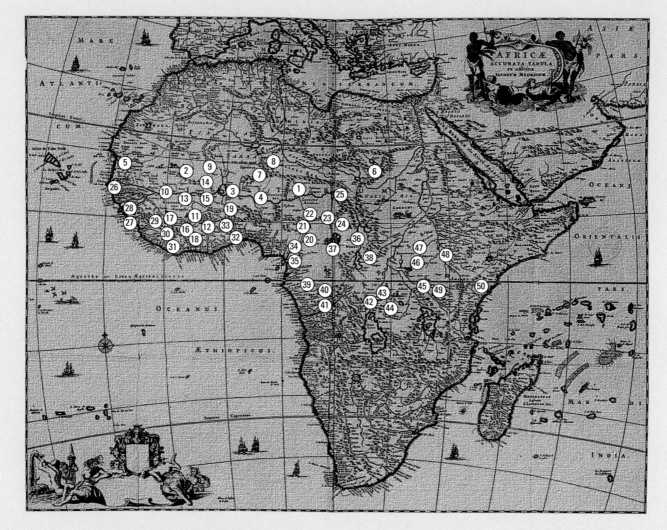

## Saharan and Northern Sahelian Zones:

1. BORORO-FULANI (NIGER)
2. SONGHAY (MALI)
3. JERMA (NIGER)
4. HAUSA (NIGERIA)
5. MOORS (MAURITANIA)
6. TEDA-DAZA (CHAD)
7. BELLAH (NIGER)
8. TUAREG (NIGER)

## Western Dry Savanna and Southern Sahel:

9. DOGON (MALI)
10. BAMBARA (MALI)
11. BOBO (BURKINA FASO)
12. BWA (BURKINA FASO)
13. SAMO (BURKINA FASO)
14. KURUMBA (BURKINA FASO)
15. MOSSI (BURKINA FASO)
16. SENUFO (IVORY COAST)
17. MALINKE (IVORY COAST)
18. DYULA (IVORY COAST)
19. SOMBA (BENIN)
20. FALI (CAMEROON)
21. KAPSIKI (CAMEROON)
22. MATAKAM (CAMEROON)
23. MUSA (CHAD)
24. SARA (CHAD)
25. DANDALEAT (CHAD)

## Atlantic Coast and Western Wooded Savanna:

26. DIOLA (SENEGAL)
27. NALU (GUINEA)
28. BAGA (GUINEA)
29. KONO (GUINEA)
30. DAN-YAKUBA (IVORY COAST)
31. WÈ (IVORY COAST)
32. FON (BENIN)
33. YORUBA (BENIN)

## Central and East Africa:

34. BAMUM (CAMEROON)
35. BAMILEKE (CAMEROON)
36. BANDA (CENTRAL AFRICAN REPUBLIC)
37. GBAYA (CENTRAL AFRICAN REPUBLIC)
38. NGBAKA (CENTRAL AFRICAN REPUBLIC/ZAIRE)
39. NJABI (GABON)
40. KUYU (REPUBLIC OF CONGO)
41. TEKE (REPUBLIC OF CONGO)
42. PENDE (ZAIRE)
43. KUBA (ZAIRE)
44. SALAMPASU (ZAIRE)
45. KOMO (ZAIRE)
46. MBUTI (ZAIRE)
47. MANGBETU (ZAIRE)
48. ALUR (ZAIRE)
49. TUTSI (RWANDA)
50. MASAI (TANZANIA)

*Michel Huet in 1950, seated beside a traditional chief*

# Foreword

The liberation of France in 1945 had a particular meaning for me, as I imagine it did for many people of my generation. At last we had regained our freedom, we were going to be able to live, to embark on new enterprises, make new discoveries . . .

As a young professional photographer in love with adventure, I felt that the world was my oyster. I had always been keen on discovery: of virgin territories, ancient civilizations, customs and ways of life different from our own – of beauty in all its forms. I had the feeling that our industrial age would have fatal repercussions for countries that had not yet caught up with our 'progress' and that I had to start capturing – and perhaps saving – in photography those values at risk of disappearing or being transformed. But which countries should I choose? South America, Asia, Africa – I was attracted by them all.

It was quite by chance, while I was doing an article on the Museum of African Art, that the process got under way. The African atmosphere in the curator's office, where I conducted the preliminary interview, soon captivated me and opened up new horizons. Then, in the museum itself, the floodlit masks and statuettes came to life. They seemed to have a message for me. I found their beauty, their harmony, quite extraordinary. I could sense the respect the sculptor had felt for his work, which he had executed in a religious trance. Unfamiliar names began to dance before my eyes: who were these mysterious Fang, Baoulé, Senufo and Bambara people who moved me to this extent? A dialogue began between myself and these masks, compelling me to find answers in the regions themselves. In other words, I had completely fallen under the spell of Africa.

There was to be no question of ethnology. I leave it to scholars to make exact, comparative studies of every ethnic group: I was, I think, an all-rounder. From Senegal to the Congo Basin, from the sand dunes of the Sahel to the Bight of Benin, through

*Map showing location of population groups referred to in the text. Countries in brackets refer to the places where photographs were taken. The terms in the vernacular languages have been transcribed into simplified forms.*
*(Translator's note: The English spellings of proper names adopted throughout are those normally used in English by Africanists – DSB.)*

thorny bush or sweltering forests, I absorbed the African land-scape without preference or prejudice. To get the feel of it, then translate it into pictures, was my aim. I soon realized that in these places music and dance were not merely entertainment but were the very expression of all that makes up the fabric of African life. Whether at weddings, funerals, harvesting or initiation, every-thing is enacted to the beat of the drums, to the sound of cow-bells and horns; everything can be interpreted according to the arrival of certain masks and following a ceremony that has remained unchanged for centuries. I also realized that I must intervene very judiciously, not disturbing the peasants during their work in the fields, but trying to be on the spot at the right moment – as a general rule, during the dry season. At this time, the village is approachable. Once the crops needed for daily sub-sistence have been gathered, the people have time to think about initiation ceremonies, to fulfil their duties to the souls of their ancestors or to give funerary honours to a dead chief. The per-formance of certain rites was essential; thus, the Baoulé needed to pour a bottle of palm wine over Queen Pokou's grave in order to consult her spirit. Consent was given for this.

Sometimes African prohibitions extended to us, and if women were forbidden to lay eyes on certain masks, no exception could be made for my wife. I must add that though she was occasion-ally excluded on this account, she made up for it elsewhere with a vengeance, namely in Northern Cameroon in a village that until then had had no road suitable for vehicles, so the inhabitants had not seen a white woman in living memory. They were in ecstasy; the women squatted around her in a circle and made ono-matopoeic noises of praise and delight through their lip orna-ments. Moreover, she was made most welcome wherever she went; some children even learned her name and she became 'Mama Ghislaine' for many of them.

But to come back to the dance, the preparations, the unforeseen obstacles. We had very high expectations of Benin, in the very heart of Yoruba country, but found that for months there had been a total suspension of all dancing in the village, which had not paid its taxes and was not in a position to do so. Endless discussions followed; delicate negotiations worthy of the finest diplomats gave the village chief the idea that the dance would lead to a gift, and the gift possi-bly to a tax settlement. In short, we got the dance, the Yoruba got the gift, the administration got its taxes. Occasionally the costumes were a problem. In one place, the dances had fallen into abeyance and the costumes had been thrown away. No matter, we could wait, and the village set to work enthusiastically cutting out fabric and skins, then decorating them with cowrie shells, monkey's hair or vegetable fibres to restore the past splendour. In Burkina Faso, it was most impressive to see the inhabitants setting off at dawn to pick the soft green leaves of the shea tree for the dancers' costumes. According to tradition, every single costume had to be completely covered, so an enormous number of leaves had to be collected.

Gradually the participants arrive. In the highlands of Northern Cameroon, long lines of Fali stretch out along the mountainsides and converge on the dance-tree; the neighbouring villages empty – the forest itself allows the sacred wood to part and let its secrets filter through. The mask emerges surrounded by the musicians. The elders assemble, the children grow impatient, the first beat of the tomtom is heard . . .

Slowly, the dance takes shape. Everyone assumes his allotted place in these collective ceremonies; it is rare for any one dancer to star. Only the masks – with no one knowing whom they hide – take a leading part; although they, too, must obey the dance leader and the rhythm that the music will gradually impose on him.

These were unforgettable moments of grace. I was every-where at once, climbing on any available object to get a view of the whole scene, forcing my way into a group to catch a particu-lar movement. In fact I was much more energetic than the dancers themselves, and I have to admit that my enthusiasm always proved infectious. At first I amused them, then I inspired them with extra energy. We were caught up in the same *élan*, and suddenly the dancers stopped seeing me as 'the stranger'; they accepted me completely or perhaps forgot me, but the truth of the dance became obvious.

During this time, my wife tried to collect as much information as possible. This was not easy; a European mind cannot readily find its way through the maze of organization of the different African peoples composed of numerous ethnic groups. What is more, you cannot express in a few sentences the outward appear-ance of an infinitely profound reality whose roots go back to the beginning of time. African politeness inclines towards approval of everything and, whether out of simplicity or cunning, Africans always answered in the affirmative, both to a suggestion and to its opposite.

The whole thing would end in the ceremony of gifts (new banknotes), either given to the chief, who distributed them, or, as was the custom, planted in the women's headdresses. We would part very good friends, with many promises to return, promises we kept as my journeys took me back to visit certain groups time and time again, always pursuing a particular inter-est, looking for a new discovery.

What can I suggest to those who would like to rediscover this Africa, or at least see for themselves a part of what I had the good fortune to get to know, and to do this in spite of the very difficult conditions that hang heavy over the continent today and do not favour journeys and encounters? . . . First of all, one must under-stand that Africa does not surrender herself easily. The demand-ing traveller must bide his time, take the old forgotten paths, adapt to the rhythm of the country and, above all, be conscious of the Africans themselves, their dignity and their philosophy. In short, one must set out with an open mind.

*Michel Huet*

*Dance of Kapsiki women in Rumsiki (Cameroon). This photograph was taken in the 1950s and now has archival value, since only the Rumsiki Peak in the background remains unchanged.*

# Introduction

Most African countries gained their independence more than thirty years ago. It is political independence, to be sure, but it has not been as complete as some had once imagined. Furthermore, the changeover was not painless, and the young African states experienced crises and tragedies that, unfortunately, continue to afflict them in the present day, resulting in an escalation of suffering and terrible losses for the inhabitants.

There are many reasons for this situation and they are not simply those stemming from the after-effects of colonialism. For students of political science, for example, it is important to understand that there are in Africa two parallel and apparently contradictory systems. The first, based on the Western model in the form of a republic with a constitution, laws and army, often rests on a colonial and mainly bureaucratic foundation. The second system tries to continue the old tribal structures, which were already pretty well transformed during the colonial period but which, nevertheless, retain some dominant features, particularly with regard to the power of the chiefs and the clans. As these two systems cannot be combined, the result is often a confused situation in which vote-rigging, nepotism and corruption predominate.

Naturally, this situation could only have a negative effect on the introduction of development policies, and it is surprising that more importance has not been attached to this phenomenon. But it must not be forgotten that in Africa a strong relationship exists between the individual and his cultural environment. The very term 'individual' hardly seems appropriate here, as everyone is part of a group – the extended family, the village community or urban district – or else belongs to one or other of the many associations, whether ethnic in origin or not, such as age groups, *tontines* (groups of people who contribute to a common fund that is paid out to each member in turn), secret societies, and so on. It is a grave mistake to ignore this sense of collectivity or this network of cultural inter-relationships, and this partly explains the repeated failures of a development policy that is conceived and imposed from the outside without reference to the African cultural environment.

In 1988, the United Nations proclaimed a Decade of Cultural Development, stating, 'It is difficult to imagine programmes of development being drawn up without taking into account the diversity of cultures and the cultural interaction of the inhabitants of different countries or regions of the world,' and adding, 'the first aim of this Decade is to convince the decision-makers to take effective account of human factors' (UNESCO, 1988: 19).

Thus, one of the first tasks – long and difficult as it may prove – is to understand what these human factors represent, and to analyse them with all the scientific rigour they deserve. Indeed, too often relegated to the rank of folklore or occasional manifestations, ancient African cultures often have been disregarded. Yet they still constitute the

*Dance of young Banda girls during the Gaza initiation rite (Central African Republic)*

expression of the identity of the African peoples and of their integration into society, even for those who reject or fight them in the name of progress or a political ideology, or from ignorance, as in the case of westernized town-dwellers or those who call themselves 'emancipated'. 'Culture is what remains when the rest has been forgotten . . . or lost'. The saying is particularly apt today, when Africa is experiencing unprecedented economic and political stagnation that holds tragic consequences for most of its inhabitants.

## The Illustrations

The illustrations in this book make their own original contribution to the understanding of African culture. They effectively serve as invaluable visual archives, since not only the natural settings but also the people and the scenes featured in the photographs have all but disappeared, or exist only in very different forms. The first photos, in fact, were taken just after the end of the Second World War, during a time that marked a turning point in African history, the period just preceding decolonization and continuing well after the euphoria of independence. It was also an epoch of African renaissance, during which emerged such great names in science, literature, the arts and politics, as Cheikh Anta Diop, Léopold Sédar Senghor, Amadou Hampâté Bâ, Félix Eboué and Kwame N'Krumah, among others.

These pictures not only have a great aesthetic quality, but must also be considered for their value as testimony. Even if, for the most part, they only refer to the Francophone countries of Africa, this testimony is now irreplaceable, particularly for new African generations who did not know the period in question. For, paradoxically, while our modern society has at its disposal the most rapid and sophisticated means of communication, the spread of knowledge is becoming more and more difficult. There is scarcely time to study anything thoroughly; the most urgent matters must be attended to first, and so often what does not seem essential must be sacrificed. But who can say what is essential if one has not taken the time to learn?

Michel Huet, for his part, has taken his time. Naturally he does not claim to have worked scientifically, and there is no question of this being a sort of American-style visual anthropology that makes a vain attempt to forget the presence of the camera and the cameraman, who centres his picture and chooses his viewpoint. Of course it is quite normal to doubt the validity of the photographs. Were the scenes not set up by the photographer? Did he not choose them according to personal criteria?

But the authenticity of the images in these pictures is certain. For those who really know Africa, there are signs that cannot deceive; for example, the spontaneity, the harmony of movements and gestures, even the expressions on the faces. After all, it is not difficult to recognize the differences between a 'posed' photograph and one taken from life.

If the sequence of the illustrations in this book are in the main the result of the publisher's decision, it nevertheless follows a certain ethnological pattern. The documents, which refer to fifty groups or peoples, have been divided into four chapters, according to geography, and correspond roughly to the zones Michel Huet travelled through in the course of his many African voyages.

Madimba *(seventeen-barred xylophones) in the curved shape typical of the Lunda, being played by Pende men (Zaire)*

The majority of the photos bear witness in fact to the most profound and mysterious elements in African culture – those concerning ritual activities especially – and the information given is based on the most recent ethnographic research.

# Ritualistic Africa

L.-V. Thomas and R. Luneau (1969) defined the African as 'incurably religious', and they might have added 'and, above all, a ritualist'. The difference between the two expressions is, admittedly, not very great, it is mainly a question of degree. Whereas the former refers to religion in general as a system of beliefs, the second is more concerned with the practical performance of rites, that is, acts prescribed by religion to attain its objectives. It is in the latter sense that the meaning of the gestures, attitudes, symbols and other manifestations of a religious nature, as revealed by the illustrations in this book, will be dealt with.

Ritual activities still form an integral part of African cultures, and give them their true dimension, even though great changes have occurred since these pictures were taken. Contrary to certain received ideas, African traditions are not fixed, and they have often been adapted to new living conditions. Even today, in spite of enormous difficulties – and possibly even because of them – rites and sacrifices are still performed, not only in the rural areas but also in the towns, as a means of overcoming daily problems, suffering and the malaise that mostly arises from an inability to adapt to foreign ways of life. The rites, then, fulfil a psycho-therapeutic function, enabling the equilibrium that is disturbed by death, illness, economic and social difficulties, and so forth, to be restored. The ritual phenomenon is also spreading increasingly, among Catholics, Muslims and especially in the independent churches, or sects, which have multiplied alarmingly in Africa.

Admittedly, there are different categories of rites, according to regions, peoples, religious systems and their mythological foundations, and also their aims. In fact, it is nearly always a question of a collective activity, something that goes beyond the individual and concerns his extended family as well as his neighbours, members of his age group or the association to which he belongs.

## Seasonal rites

However, there are rites that regularly involve the whole village community; these are the seasonal rites performed in the rural areas, in particular the harvest festivals. But they can occur before the field work begins, especially in an effort to bring rain and, above all, to cleanse the earth of the impurities with which man has defiled it in the course of the year. Indeed, the African peasant well knows from experience that his labours and knowledge are not always sufficient to ensure good harvests. The rain must still be abundant and must come at the right time, the plants must not be destroyed by disease, insects or other predators. With this aim in view, they attempt to conciliate the spiritual forces that control these phenomena, as well as the ancestors – the most important intermediaries – and, at the same

Yoke *mask of the Baga from the Lower Guinea Coast. As imposing as the celebrated* Nimba *mask, the* Yoke *is linked more to the theme of maternity, whereas the* Nimba *seems to symbolize fertile soil and abundant crops.*

time, to settle differences within the family or the village. This is the case with the rites that precede the work in the fields, as performed by the Bwa and the Bobo in Burkina Faso, who use masks made from *Do* leaves. It is also true of the rites for the first yam crop, which are observed by the Akan peoples (Ashanti, Agni, Baoulé, etc.) of the Ivory Coast and Ghana, and by the Ewe of Togo. The rite for the first crops has retained a certain importance, as it announces the beginning of the traditional or ritual year, while it also expresses renewal and strength, symbolized by the appearance of the first fruits. Thus, among the Yoruba people of Etiki in Nigeria, the rite of the first yam crop used to usher in a period of licence that ended with demonstrations of strength by the young men of the locality, who would wear very heavy masks. The Fon of Benin still associate the festival of the first crop of millet with the annual rituals of the former royalty and the voodoo pantheon.

## Rites of passage

This expression refers to rites that mark the passage from one stage of existence to another, beginning with the rites performed following the birth, the conferring of the name on the child, and the mother's rising from childbed. Then there is the initiation, marking the passage from childhood to adulthood, the rites of betrothal and marriage and, finally, the burial rites, which enable the deceased to join the ranks of the ancestors.

Initiation rites, which aim to transform young persons – girls and boys, or boys or girls only, according to the region – into adults, are the most spectacular and are, in any case, those that make the strongest impression on Europeans, particularly because of the circumcision of boys and excision of girls, or other painful ordeals. This interest explains the frequent misinterpretation. However, schooling, 'modernization' and the drift from the land, are all much more responsible for the decline of these traditions than the anathema of the colonials. Nowadays initiation exists only in isolated areas and then in a very watered-down form: the length of time spent in the 'bush camps' has been reduced and these take place more and more during the school holidays; excision has been abandoned except in certain Muslim regions; and the instruction of young people has been radically simplified. Formerly, this

*Dance of the* Gazawoko *girls, initiates of the* Gaza *rites practised by the Ngbaka people (Central African Republic/Zaire)*

Bwoom *or* Mboom *mask, in the Royal Museum of Central Africa, Terfuren. According to the tradition of the Bushong, who form the nucleus of the Kuba people in Zaire, this mask is said to have been revealed to King Miko mi Mbul by the Tswa Pygmies.*

learning included, *inter alia*, knowledge of the environment, introduction to farming techniques, the group's history and its spiritual foundations, the history of the lineages – in short, the oral history of the society – as well as advice on marriage. All of this is done, of course, in a very different manner from the teaching in 'White' schools, employing very specific memorization exercises, using proverbs and riddles, for example, or cultural symbols such as masks and sacred objects, and through songs and dances. The end of the young people's initiation and their return to the village is always the occasion for a great celebration during which the masks representing the tutelary heroes and other mythical characters appear. These masks, which are part of the history of the group and its natural environment, are the principal actors in what can be called a veritable local religion. They form a sort of chain that links the visible and invisible worlds, the world of today with that of its origins, the living and the dead, natural and spiritual forces.

The ancestors play an important part in this chain, for they act as mediators between the different worlds. So one must petition them to intercede in favour of their descendants. But, in order for the deceased to join the ranks of the ancestors, funeral rites are essential. These take place over long periods and are often a heavy burden on the family. First of all, it is necessary to 'expel death' from the group of the living, for death is contagious in Africa! This is the rite of separation or the actual interment. Then the spirit or the soul of the deceased must be settled in the world of the dead; this is the rite of integration. And, finally, a lasting relationship must be established with the deceased by means of objects, for example; this is the rite of consecration.

## Rites associated with power

In some regions chiefdoms still exist. These are systems of government dating from the pre-colonial era, which have naturally lost their erstwhile power, but which play as important a part as they did in the past and even continue to fill a certain political role, albeit in different ways. This is particularly the case in Anglophone Africa. In Nigeria, for example, the descendants of the former Yoruba royal family still have some political and economic power. Elsewhere, the representatives of the old chiefdoms are restricted to their ritual roles, but that comes to the same thing in practice, given the importance of ritual in Africa.

The role of the chief – the favoured intermediary between the ancestors, the natural forces and the people – is most evident in Cameroon. For example, the Bamileke chiefdoms are organized into something like a 'community enterprise', with the chief sharing out the profits by distributing the fields and the resources of the secret societies among the members of the chiefdom. He relies, in fact, on these secret societies who lend him their support, either financially or by their services (maintenance of order, upkeep of hedges, arranging ceremonies for the souls of the ancestors, etc.). Moreover, the chief does not govern alone; he must surround himself with influential counsellors recruited from his own family and from among the ordinary members of the chiefdom. The secret societies also have their say. The most prestigious among them demand very high import duties indeed, which are shared with the chief and the elders. So there exists a certain spirit of economic competitiveness, which naturally contributes to the success of the Bamileke outside the chiefdom.

## Ritualistic symbols

There are many symbols used in the course of rituals: masks, costumes, musical instruments, particular objects (fly-whisks, amulets, magical objects, etc.), a whole battery of equipment, charged with meaning, that must be analysed if the true scope of the ritual is to be understood.

The masks, for example, introduce characters drawn from the village society or the bush, and are used to depict

*Procession of girls initiated in the Gaza rites coming to the water hole to collect water for the ritual bath, Gbaya (Central African Republic)*

the principal episodes from the myth of creation and the history of the group through the oral tradition. The masks represent humans or animals and are often hybrid forms. They are worn in front of the face or on top of the head, the wearer being hidden under a costume which forms an integral part of the mask (as do his own voice, his miming, his dance or his attitude). It is difficult to find the true meaning of a mask of which only the carved wooden part survives, hence the importance of the photographs showing the masks 'in action'.

Musical instruments can also reveal the meaning of the ritual, since there are instruments reserved for particular masks, or particular phases of the ritual. Drums (with membranes or with slits), which are carved out of tree trunks, not only lend their rhythm to the dance, but enable messages to be transmitted through their beat. The other objects – statuettes, thrones, fabrics, utensils – that appear on these occasions, also help to give a certain meaning to the ritual.

Finally, one must not forget the very active participation of the onlookers who accompany the dances with singing or clapping, thus introducing a dialogue with the actors in what can be called a 'ritual ballet'.

*This 'elephant-mask', consisting of a long hood and huge ears and decorated with multicoloured beads,*
*is characteristic of a Bamileke secret society in West Cameroon, to whom it is unique.*

# CHAPTER ONE

# Saharan and Northern Sahelian Zones

On maps, the vast expanse of the Sahara Desert is shown as a huge empty area, traditionally made still more explicit by being coloured yellow. But it was not always thus; less than one thousand years ago the Sahara was still a grassy region with excellent pasturelands, abundant game, and springs and rivers well stocked with fish, as shown in the Tassili n'Ajjer rock paintings.

Since then the desert has advanced unremittingly towards the south, more than one hundred km in the last twenty years. Repeated droughts are not the only cause; man has been largely responsible for creating the desert through overgrazing, the absence of a proper agricultural policy of irrigation and soil conservation, the felling of trees for firewood, and through armed conflicts, etc. To the south of this zone is the beginning of the Sahel (from an Arabic word which, in fact, refers to a coastal region, the shore!). In reality, the northern part of the Sahel is nowadays scarcely distinguishable from the Sahara, and consists of similar sandy, waterless areas. Yet some peoples still cling to these awe-inspiring if desolate landscapes, like the Tuaregs, who, as a consequence of the drought, which lasted from 1973 to 1983 and resulted in the loss of their flocks, were forced to abandon their former nomadic life. Nevertheless, however inhospitable it may be, the Sahara has been an important transit route, thanks to the camel (or dromedary) – the veritable ship of the desert. For centuries, caravans crossed the desert in every direction, transporting natron from the saltpans in the south, dates from the oases in the north, manufactured goods from North Africa and the east, and, in the past, slaves and gold destined for Egypt and the Arab world. The traffic was very intense until the end of the last century and it brought fame to cities such as Timbuktu and Jenne in Mali, Agades in Niger and Walata in Mauritania, among others.

*Herald, belonging to the retinue of a Hausa emir, blowing the* kakaki *horn (Nigeria)*

# The Bororo Fulani

## Niger (Dakoro area)

Yake *dance*

For the nomadic Fulani the period of festivities begins with the first rains, when the flocks have returned from the salt pastures. Then they meet in *worso* – gatherings of descendants of the same lineage – and the young people perform mating dances such as the *Yake*, and the *Gereol (Gerewol* or *Geraoul)*. In fact, the Bororo people, and the nomadic Fulani in general, worship physical beauty in both humans and animals. They have many songs praising the merits of

a particular slender-waisted *jijiru* girl, some bright-eyed shepherd, or the cow with the light coat, which gives the best milk in the region.

The *Yake*, as distinct from the *Gereol*, is danced at gatherings of one specific lineage. The *Gereol* is the name given not only to a particular dance but to a very large-scale tribal ceremony, common to the Wodaabe and Bororo nomadic tribes, which brings together members of many lineages

and is the means of asserting affiliation to a specific bloodline. The *Yake* dance (the name signifies 'comrades of the same age group') brings together young people of both sexes, often already married, who form two lines, with boys on one side and girls on the other. Each takes his or her place in the line according to age and bloodline, so as to face a partner from the most distant lineage to their own.

The dance consists of several stages. First of all, the boys stand close together, swaying from one foot to the other, while singing and clapping. They have dressed for the occasion in their finest apparel, wearing all sorts of jewellery and amulets, as well as carrying their weapons. As they dance, they roll their eyes and keep up a permanent smile to show off the whiteness of their pupils and their teeth. The girls, meanwhile, dance gracefully towards them in pairs.

The girls have been chosen for their beauty by the *sami*, the team leader, and they wave their arms towards the boys who please them most. In this way they pair off and retire discreetly into the darkness of the night, giving rise to more or less lasting liaisons, a sort of secondary marriage, on the understanding that the young women who take part in the *Yake* dance are still childless.

*Court musicians at Gao*

These young women, wearing the elaborate Fulani hair-style, decorated with amber and beads, are playing two instruments widely used in all the encampments of the Sahel nomads.

The first, called an *inzad*, is a one-stringed hurdy-gurdy. The sound-box is made from half a calabash over which a goat skin is stretched. A wooden handle is fixed across this 'table' enabling the horsehair string to be attached. The bow is a simple curved stick with a string also made of horsehair. This instrument is capable of a great range of effects, being able, for example, to imitate the human voice, which is why it is often favoured by West African storytellers and *griots* (singers, chroniclers, genealogists).

Among the Tuareg, the same type of instrument is used to accompany the songs at the 'court of love'. The other instrument, a hemispherical drum with the membrane tied over it, is similar to the Tuareg *tobol*.

# The Jerma (Zarma)

## Niger (Filingué region)

*Procession of horsemen*

The Jerma, also known as Zarma or Zerma, descendants of the former conquerors from Mali, have become fairly closely linked with the Songhay, whose language they share.

The Jerma have gained a reputation as warriors and horsemen that the local *griots* perpetuate in the many epic tales from their repertoire. The Jerma are also known as excellent weavers, and their elaborate fabrics are in great demand in West Africa.

The traditions linked to the time when the Jerma warlords roamed the area have been particularly well preserved in the Filingué region and are occasionally revived in processions of horsemen, armed from head to foot like the knights of old, wearing helmets, carrying decorative parade spears, and mounted on horses caparisoned in rich fabrics.

*Songhay dance at the gates of Gao (Mali)*

## Mauritania (Nema region)

According to geographers, Mauritania is one vast desert, the western region of the Sahara, which even stretches in some places to the shores of the Atlantic. Partly as the result of the vagaries of climate and, equally dramatically, the work of man himself, the country's only sources of subsistence are its mineral deposits, animal husbandry – a practice that is doomed – and fishing. And yet, in former times considerable herds roamed over a large part of the country: camels in the north and centre, where the grazing was scarce, and cattle, goats and sheep in the south, where grasslands were more plentiful. This was the land of the Hassans, or Hassania, descendants of warrior tribes from Morocco, who invaded Mauritania between the fifteenth and sixteenth centuries. Thus, the Berber origin of the Moors should predominate, but, as with the Tuareg, the reality is complicated by numerous extraneous elements, Arab and African.

*Dance of the women*

# The Hausa

## Nigeria

*Mounted musicians in an emir's retinue*

Among the majority of Islamic peoples of Western Africa, considerable chiefdoms survive, integrated into the national political structures, with emirs or sultans at their head. To enhance their prestige, these traditional chiefs surround themselves with a large retinue of followers, a veritable court, in fact, with its etiquette and regular musicians. In the case of the Hausa of Northern Nigeria, the emirs and sultans still occupy key positions between the people and the local authorities. On the occasion of a national holiday or the visit of an official personage the emirs organize parades and processions accompanied by

their own bands. These generally consist of iron or brass trumpets, called *kakaki*, which are at least three metres long and are sometimes fitted with a double horn or bell, as shown in the photograph on the opposite page. The *kakaki* trumpet serves to announce an important arrival, and its peals accentuate the sound of the *alghaita* (single-reed oboes, played like bagpipes), which are generally accompanied by several drums.

# The Daza (Gorane)

## Chad (Fada region, Ennedi)

*Dance of the women*

The Teda and Daza form a homogenous ethnic group known as the Tubu. They are scattered over the vast Tibesti. The Daza are called *Gor'an* by the Arabs, and their origin is debateable. They are supposed to be the distant descendants of 'white' nomads from the Valley of the Nile who settled among the indigenous black inhabitants.

The migratory Teda-Daza live mostly on animal husbandry and precarious farming; formerly they were fearsome warriors who indulged in raids to seize slaves and livestock. The women of this region wear loose cotton garments and pull a flap of the skirt over their heads to form a sort of hood to shield themselves from the sun. They wear heavy silver anklets and necklaces of large amber beads, as well as a silver nose ring in one nostril, which is pierced when a girl is seven; her lips and gums are tattooed black when she is twelve. Nowadays the Teda-Daza are Muslims and practise marriage rites similar to those of Arabs, accompanied by celebrations with dancing and singing to the beat of the drums. In certain places the bride is brought with a large retinue to her husband's home, mounted on a camel and hidden under a tall canopy decorated with her kitchen utensils.

## The Tuareg

*Dance of the Bellah women*

### Niger (Agadès region)

*Tuareg chiefs from the Ahir region*

The Tuareg, of Berber origin, settled in the Sahara in the eleventh century, under pressure from Arab invaders such as the Beni Hilal. For centuries they were the lords of the desert, leaving the black inhabitants, whom they had subdued, to look after the herds of camels and flocks of goats and sheep; for the Tuareg's main occupation at the time was carrying out raids and taking part in seasonal festivities that gave them the opportunity of showing themselves off to advantage and indulging in the 'court of love'. At that time, the Tuaregs had a feudal society consisting of nobles (*Imageren*), free men (*Imrad*) and marabouts educated in the Muslim religion (*Ineslemen*), who represented the actual Tuareg people. Besides these, there were two other inferior classes: the smiths (*Inaden*), mainly of Hausa origin, and the Bellah, servants or former tributaries of the Tuareg.

At one time very proud of their nomadic existence and even exhibiting a certain contempt for farming and sedentary folk in general, the Tuareg still show traces of a former matriarchal system, which possibly derives from the legend that the Hoggar Tuareg trace their origins to a female ancestor, Tin Hinan. Hints of this system can be found in certain forms of succession, although that is normally based on the Arab model of paternal lineage. Also, in accordance with their Berber origin, the Tuareg preferred to elect their chiefs from an inferior class, so as to avoid the office passing from father to son. Long under the domination of the Tuareg, the Agadès region is now inhabited by a number of settled black peoples, who were formerly continuously subject to the Tuareg's demands and provided the main body of 'tent captives'. It was from among these that the Tuaregs selected their female musicians.

# CHAPTER TWO

# Western Dry Savanna and Southern Sahel

Situated to the south and west of the previous zone, these arid regions are characterized by grassy savanna lands planted with palmyras and shea trees. Millet is by far the principal subsistence crop, although in certain areas fonio and sorghum come a close second, and sometimes cash crops such as groundnuts, and especially cotton, are grown. The farmers here are the most determined and resourceful in all Africa, as the only available land is poor, and threatened by the constant encroachment of laterite. Outstanding among them are the Bambara, the Dogon and the Senufo. Since the terrible droughts of 1973 to 1983, it has also become a region of animal husbandry, and this has resulted in friction between the nomadic herdsmen and sedentary farmers. A more effective occupancy of the land and a better association between livestock and agriculture would no doubt give rise to improved yields and better neighbourliness! The eleventh- and twelfth-century Arab chroniclers called this zone *Bilal es Sudan*, 'the land of the black people'. Dazzled by the gold disbursed by the Emperor of Mali during his pilgrimage to Mecca in 1324, other Arab travellers journeyed through this part of West Africa. They have left us such invaluable reports as Ibn Batouta's account of the former Mali empire, written about 1350. In this way, we know about the old empires of the Songhay, of Ghana and of the Mossi, as well as the rich Hausa city-states, such as Kano, the kingdoms of the Kanem-Borno and of the Fulani of Macina. The Western savanna is, then, a part of Africa that is rich in history, where cultural traditions have been preserved thanks to the *griots*, the real West African historiographers. But one must not forget the heavy toll taken by the slave trade, particularly with regard to the inhabitants of Mande, and later by colonization, with its forced labour, and by the world wars of 1914–18 and 1939–45.

*Yagule* mask, with which the Dogon of Mali satirize certain types of women, especially the Fulani

# The Dogon

## Mali (Sangha region)

*Masks emerging from their hiding places in the rocks*

The celebrated Bandiagara cliffs are riddled with caves and crevices, and it is here that masks are fashioned, where they can be hidden from prying eyes. In the past, non-initiates, especially women, were forbidden to view them, and a *rhombe* (an instrument made from a thin piece of wood, which is shaken violently to produce a sort of whirring sound) was used to warn of the masks' approach. These masks were not intended to last very long, and once they had served their purpose, they were simply abandoned in the caves.

Sirige *mask*

This mask can easily reach a height of three metres, and is without doubt one of the most impressive in the whole of West Africa. The part covering the face is rectangular, as is the case with most Dogon masks, and above this is a tall wooden board carved into holes of various shapes and decorated with geometric designs. The term *sirige* refers to the houses of more than one storey that used to be reserved for the chiefs, or *hogon*.

This mask can be interpreted as encapsulating the mythical story of mankind, from the time of the descent to earth

over an archway – which is suggested by the structure of the *ginna* (the family home) – as well as the succession of generations. In his day, Marcel Griaule recorded the different myths relating to the *Sirige*. He thought that its shape was somehow based on that of the great mask, sometimes known as 'the mother-mask', carved for a *Sigui*, the initiation ceremony that takes place every fifty or sixty years. According to the mythology, a young goatherd came upon a group of Andumbulu as they were holding a meeting in the bush, and so discovered the shape of the mask, a long piece of wood, which the Andumbulu broke before they fled.

The Dogon living in the Bandiagara cliff region have probably been better documented than any other of the Sahel peoples. It can even be said that the French ethnological school developed from the study of these fonio growers. The smallest details are known of their rich mythology; the traditions linked to their masks, initiation and funeral rites have been the subjects of scholarly works since their arts were first reported on by Marcel Griaule and his assistants at the time of the famous Dakar-Djibouti mission in 1933. Naturally, it was the masks brought out for funerals that originally attracted attention because of their spectacular appearance and almost surreal shapes. It must be remembered, in fact, that funeral rites are extremely important to the Dogon, not only those that accompany the actual interment, but especially the ceremonies that mark the close of the mourning period, known as *Dama*. If the deceased was

a notable person, it was an occasion for bringing out the masks to be worn by the initiated members of the *Awa*, the brotherhood of the masks. The latter re-enact in human and animal forms the great moments of their mythical history.

*Masks dancing in Sangha*

The Dogon masked dances have become very famous. These take place not only at the time of the *Dama*, but are also performed for the benefit of visiting tourists. Nevertheless, the traditional format is fairly well preserved, and the masks still fulfil their role of handing down the oral traditions by presenting different types of characters drawn from mythology or from Dogon society (the smith, Fulani women, etc.).

*The* Kanaga *mask*

The *Kanaga* mask is undoubtedly the most easily recognizable of all the Dogon masks because of its superstructure, which resembles the cross of Lorraine. It is also one of the most important for its symbolism. For the lay person, the vertical piece of wood, with its cross-bars at top and bottom, is the stylized representation of a sort of bird; while, for the initiated, it symbolizes man's presence between heaven and earth. The *Kanaga* mask lends itself to other interpretations. For example, it could serve to

Kanaga *mask*

illustrate the theme of the archway, which reached the earth in the form of a woman and brought the various seeds that enabled man to live on earth, thanks to the smith who taught their use. Finally, some see this mask as representing *Ogo*, the white fox to whom the Dogon attribute mankind's first misfortunes.

*Dogon 'thieves' crooks' (*yo dommolo*). The clans' ritual 'thieves' display their crooks during the funeral of one of their members, Sangha (Mali)*

# The Bambara (Baumana)

## Mali (Segu and Buguni regions)

The Bambara or Baumana (more correctly Banmana) are descended from the Mande group of peoples, but contrary to the other subdivisions of this group, the Malinke for example, they have always resisted Islam, at least until very recently. Indeed, that is why their Muslim neighbours called them *Banmana* or *Bambara*, which means 'infidels'.

More farmers than warriors, the Bambara have nevertheless known a brilliant period of history, that of the Segu kingdom, founded in the seventeenth century when the Songhay empire fell. According to legend, the kingdom was founded by Baramangolo, who crossed the River Niger on the back of a catfish at the site of the city of Segu.

Nowadays the Bambara are the most important tribe in Mali, and all hopes of ensuring the country's needs lie with them, owing to the drought which has raged for several years in the north.

Like many farming communities solidly attached to their land, the Bambara have succeeded in preserving their most important cultural traditions, in particular those concerning the family, the role of the village chiefs who represent the founding ancestors and play an active part in the agrarian rites, the system of age groups based on initiation, the brotherhoods of initiates that perpetuate these, and all cults and religious beliefs, both individual and collective.

*Masks of the* Ntomo *(or* Ndomo*), one of the six initiatory brotherhoods of the Bambara, Segu (Mali)*

Tyiwara *mask*

*Tyiwara* is the name given to one of the initiatory brotherhoods, or *dyow*. There are six of these and all play influential roles in traditional Bambara society. Each of them maintains with the others a complementary inter-relationship based on the various aspects of human existence. They form, in effect, a school of wisdom, in which man progresses along the path of knowledge. Naturally each of these brotherhoods, or stages of initiation, possesses different accessories and masks, a whole collection of symbols or connections that the initiates can recognize.

The *Tyiwara* phase, which precedes the final stage of maturity, that of *Kore*, has to do with the mastery of farming techniques. The man-principle, formed theoretically in the preceding *dyow* (*Komo*, *Nama* and *Kono* brotherhoods), is now replaced by manual work in the fields. Thus, man finds in the combination of these two aspects the source of his food supply and establishes the model for his association with woman. According to their mythology, *Tyiwara* is the name of the 'clawed creature, the totem of agriculture',

a fantastic being, half-man, half-beast, descended from the cobra and the first woman on earth. This creature taught man how to till the soil. But ungrateful man eventually ceased to respect what he had been taught, and *Tyiwara* disappeared underground. Then men had the idea of carving a mask in its likeness to perpetuate it.

The *Tyiwara* masked dancers perform as part of the agrarian rites, to ensure the success of their crops. Masks and other ritual objects then bring about a synthesis of the different elements that contribute to a successful harvest: sun, water, soil, hard work or the energy of the group of farmers.

The masks, or carved wooden superstructures, consist of animal symbols that stand for knowledge of the natural forces, for example, the antelope and the aardvark. The one here shows three antelopes, one on top of the other, two gazelles and a stylized sable antelope – animals that mainly refer to crops that grow above ground and have weak root structures, such as fonio, millet and sorrel.

# The Bobo, Bwa (Bobo Oulé)

## Burkina Faso

Only in the last few years have the Bobo Oulé been considered a separate ethnic group, that of the Bwa, as distinct from the Bobo. In fact, for a long time the Bwa and the Bobo were arbitrarily classed under the name of Bobo. However, the Bwa speak a language of Voltaic origin, whereas the Bobo are linked to the Mande group of languages. It was the Mandingoes who got into the habit of using this name when referring to the inhabitants of the Bobo-Dioulasso region, who are known as Boboy. They later qualified them as either Bobo Fing, that is, 'black Bobo' or Bobo Oulé, 'red Bobo'. These names have no real significance, they only serve to indicate two different groups that are nevertheless combined under the term Bobo, because of many cultural similarities, particularly in religious practices. Nowadays, the Bobo Fing have become the actual Bobo, and the Bobo Oulé the Bwa.

These two groups have a similar way of life that is linked to agriculture, the village, the soil and its spiritual forces. They have many cultural characteristics in common and only differ in the ways they operate. For example, the Bobo show more respect for tradition than the Bwa, who are fairly individualistic and have adopted various elements from the culture of their neighbours, in particular the Gurunsi.

Kele *masks made of plaited fibre, used by the Bobo (Bobo Fing or Bobo proper) in the* Do *or* Dwo *cult, Bobo-Dioulasso region (Burkina Faso)*

# The Samo

## Burkina Faso (village of Kiembara)

*Dance of the men of the rain clan*

The Samo of Yatenga divide the clans in every village into groups. The rain people and the soil people constitute the two dominant branches and share the ritual, judicial and social roles. Seasonal celebrations, based on the solar year, punctuate the various activities of these village communities. Two of them seem to play a particularly important part, as the renewal of the year depends on them: these are *Tièdadara* and *Tièrtaye*. The former, which takes place before the first rains, is the responsibility of the *lamutyiri*, the master of the rain, whereas the second depends on the *tudana*, the master of the soil. It must, however, be pointed out that the master of the rain has the major part to play as he is responsible for fixing the date of both ceremonies based on secret and complicated calculations; sometimes he even combines the two functions. Traditionally he is responsible for ensuring both the village welfare, which

depends on the rain – and everyone knows how important this is for the Sahelian regions which have suffered particularly from drought – and the peace, not only in the village itself but also between federate villages that share the same needs as regards defence and land use. Curiously enough, the *lamutyiri* is appointed by the *tudana* who eventually becomes, in a way, his assistant.

The master of the rain, a person considered sacred, is subjected to all kinds of prohibitions and regulations. In effect he is the intermediary between heaven and earth and he presides over the rain-making rituals 'to open the way for the rain', as they say in the area. In the course of these rituals, the dancers, wearing costumes and crested headdresses entirely covered in cowrie shells, blow long whistles and imitate the patter of the rain by means of metal rings and other sound effects.

# The Kurumba (Nioniosi)

### Burkina Faso (Aribinda region)

There has been much debate about the origin of the Kurumba. Some presume them to have come from the Dogon country, and it is true they share many cultural features. They are said to have been driven out by the Dogon, who were themselves fleeing from the Mossi and sought refuge in the Lurum region in the sixteenth century. According to others, the recent discovery of the ancient Tellem civilization, to which the Dogon are linked in their present habitat, completely refutes this hypothesis.

Be that as it may, the Kurumba consider themselves the oldest inhabitants of Yatenga and for this reason call themselves *Nioniosi*, meaning 'long established'. Like their Dogon neighbours, the Kurumba are cultivators of the dry savanna. They have a structure of traditional chiefdoms, but are also grouped into several clans that have their representatives in the various villages. The Kurumba masks, of which several types exist, are carved in honour of family, clan or village chiefs after their deaths. They do not necessarily represent the deceased, but living creatures who enhance the family prestige. The majority are richly coloured with many geometric designs that, like coats of arms, serve to identify the clan or the family to which they belong, while, at the same time, recalling the main events in their cosmogonic myth.

The collective name of the masks is *adone* or *adunei*, but each one receives its own individual name. Carved in the greatest secrecy, they are only brought out for funerals or seasonal celebrations. The antelope mask, which is more a super-structure worn on top of the head, is frequently found in the Aribinda, Belehede and Yoro regions. It belongs to the Sawadugu clan which, with the Konfe, is at the origin of the Kurumba-Nioniosi population.

*Doyo masks,
representing various types of
animals: the antelope on the
right, the wild boar on the
left, Bwa (Burkina Faso)*

*Procession of* Doyo *masks at Boni*

This type of mask is also sometimes called a 'multi-storey mask'. It consists of a sort of light wooden board above a round face with concentric eyes outlined in red on a white background. The board is decorated with a number of coloured geometric motifs, such as dotted lines, checks, zigzags, etc. It is found mostly in the southern part of the Bwa region, particularly among the Kademba, a subdivision of the Bwa. However, the odds are that they borrowed it from their Gurunsi neighbours, probably through the intermediary of the Ko, a small group linked to the Gurunsi, between Boromo and Oury.

The Bwa-Kademba have, in fact, been influenced by their eastern neighbours, the Ko, particularly in their religion. Although they still claim to be followers of *Do*, they have adopted a new cult, that of *Lane*, borrowed from the Ko. The *Lane* cult has brought the Bwa a new social classification of age groups and new socio-religious rituals that make use of the enormous 'multi-storey masks' like the ones seen here, which are generally made by the Ko. On the right can be seen an extremely tall mask, which imitates the skeleton of the mythical boa, *Baviri*, and, behind it, several 'multi-storey masks' as well as more realistic masks representing the buffalo, *Ia*.

Doyo *mask of the Bwa of Boni (Burkina Faso)*

*Mask used for entertainment by the Bobo of Dédugu (Burkina Faso)*

Accompanied by the *dumatonu* drum, the 'multi-storey masks' perform an elaborate balletic dance. The boards forming the masks are held in front of the face, while the dancers are hidden under a costume made from dyed red vegetable fibres.

Probably one of the most amazing masks is the one usually known as the butterfly or *bugudinde*, the name given it by the Gurunsi people from whom the Bwa borrowed it. It is made out of a long horizontal board that the wearer whirls round in a rapid dance.

*Dances of the* Doyo *masks at Houndé*

*Leaf mask of the Bwa people of Boni*

The *Do* or *Dwo* rite represents for the Bobo the purification of human society, intended to cleanse the harmonious natural world of the impurities or defilement that man cannot help introducing into it. According to the cosmogonic myth, the supreme god, *Wuro*, created the world and then entrusted men with the responsibility for maintaining its harmony, bequeathing to them at the time of his exile the mask of leaves known as *Sôwiyè*, a sacred character who represents *Do* and is a part of the god *Wuro*, himself. More or less the same concept is found among the Bwa, except that for them *Do* is the intermediary between *Debwenu*, the equivalent of the god *Wuro*, and men. *Do* is generally said to be both son and brother of *Debwenu*, indicating that he has something of the nature of the

*Dance of the leaf masks by the Bobo of Dédugu (Burkina Faso)*

supreme god. The Bwa associate *Do* with initiation and the formation of the age groups that are the basis of traditional society.

The leaf masks, called *siriureoro* or *boonukora*, according to the region, emerge every year, shortly before the arrival of the rains, for the ceremony of *lopôle* (purification rite of homes and men). At nightfall, the masks,

worn by recently initiated boys, sneak into the village and proceed through all the alleyways, touching the walls with their sticks and striking everyone they meet. This ritual lasts at least three days, sometimes longer when the rains are late in coming, and ends with a public dance in the village chief's field.

# The Mossi

## Burkina Faso (Kudugu)

*Red dancers*

These dancers get their name from a sort of red cotton tunic that is slit at the sides. They are thought by some to be the descendants of former Gurunsi prisoners who tended the horses of the Naba Moro, emperor of the Mossi, whose present-day representative still lives in the Wagadugu palace, and who once commanded a large court. These red dancers also possibly commemorate in their own way one of the episodes of the Mossi legend, according to which the Mossi people were formed from the union of the inhabi-

tants of the upper reaches of the Black and White Volta rivers and the 'red' horsemen from the east, possibly from Lake Chad.

Furthermore, the red dancers' leaps, to the accompaniment of the *griots'* drums, are reminiscent of prancing horses. The crest of the head ornament, which imitates a plaited horse's mane, and the fly-whisk made from long horsehairs, also contribute to this impression.

# The Senufo

## Ivory Coast
## (Sinématyali, Korbogo and Bundyali regions)

The Senufo, who are considered the best farmers in West Africa, and whose extraordinary wooden sculptures are world famous, have a social structure based on age groups. These are set up around the *Poro* initiation rite which, every seven years, re-enacts the Senufo mythical universe. The *Poro* embodies a very complex set of rites and traditions, and few people have had the opportunity of observing its various aspects. In spite of the inevitably fragmentary nature of the information collected up till now, it can nevertheless be stated that the aim of the *Poro* is to renew regularly the basic components of village society under the aegis of the goddess *Katyelo*, who represents both the earth and the mother of the village. Initiation takes place in the bush far from the dwellings, in a sacred place known as *sinzanga*.

The Senufo *Poro* initiation consists of several phases, each one corresponding to a distinct age group. First of all there is the junior class (*plaga, plawo, nyara*), or *Poro* for children aged between seven and twelve, which allows them to proceed to the next stage, that of the second age group (*tyenungo, nayogo, kwonro*) for those twelve to eighteen, which precedes the initiatory phase of the 'sacred wood' (*tyologo*). This completes the young men's training after the age of eighteen. Each of these age groups is known by different names, according to the region and the type of masks used in the course of the initiation years. For each group this period lasts seven years, but it can be reduced depending on the aptitude of the initiates. The passage from one class to another is marked by a ritual, but their accession to the last age group in the 'sacred wood', and their return at the end of the initiation naturally involves great public ceremonies, known as *Kafo*.

The *Nayogo* are part of the second age group, in which they occupy the second stage. They conclude their training by walking in procession through the village up to the dance-place. They are recognizable by their spectacular crested headdress completely covered in cowries and

*Procession of the* Nayogo *in the Sinématyali region*

*Procession of the* Tyenungo *or* Tyeleo *initiates at Sinématyali*

beads. A long tail of cowries hangs down the back and there is a hornbill's beak in front. This bird plays an important role in the *Poro* mythology.

The *Tyenungo* form the first stage of the second age group. The activities of the first two age groups are devoted to learning agricultural practices in order to provide the community with well-trained workers. In addition, these young farmers take part in agricultural competitions for the enviable title of champion (*Sambali*) and the prize of an elegant cane surmounted by a statuette.

*Masks made of coloured fabrics and fibres, guardians of the 'sacred wood'* (sinzanga*), Sinématyali*

*Initiates of the second age group at the* kwonro *stage, in Sinématyali*

The *kwonro* is the name given to the final phase of initiation for this age group and, consequently, precedes promotion to the highest class, that of the *tyologo*.

Prior to entering the 'sacred wood', the candidates, *Kwonbele*, perform in public wearing headdresses that vary according to the region. Here they are made of wood stained in red and white and are surmounted by huge ears and decorated with cowries.

Elsewhere they may assume an even more imposing appearance – in the form of boards painted in check designs or with cut-out animal motifs.

One of the most intense moments in the initiation ritual that takes place in the 'sacred wood' is certainly when the *Nasolo* mask appears. This rite is known as *Kagba*, which means 'of variegated colours', or sometimes *Porfige*,

'white *Poro*'. The literal translation of the term *Nasolo* is 'elephant-bull' or buffalo.

The *Nasolo* mask consists of a wooden armature covered with matting that is painted in geometric designs,

*Ritual greeting of the* Nasolo *mask in the presence of the former initiates of the sacred wood*

checks, circles, etc. This construction is at least one and a half metres high and can be five metres long. Two men, hidden under the matting, walk it along, one of them playing a sort of snare drum which gives off a powerful roaring noise. A wooden carving is fixed to the front of the mask representing an animal's head with long horns, similar to the *Ponyugo* mask but narrower. The *Nasolo* is attended by two hooded servants, who guide it through its manoeuvres and keep away the non-initiated who must not see the mask. It weaves its way through the sacred wood and its outskirts, following a well-defined route.

The *Nasolo* can be said to sum up the basic elements of the *Poro*, as do the different masks and accessories that give concrete expression to the various phases of the initiation ritual.

The *Nasolo* emerges from the sacred wood on the occasion of funerals of former initiates and notables, and makes its way to the village, attended by other masked characters from the *Poro*, to the sound of traditional musical instruments, such as large wooden horns (*napalenien*), long drums (*tyopigen*) and the big bass drum (*gpobinge*). No non-initiate must encounter the mask on its way. When it meets former initiates, it rears up to greet them.

*Arrival of the* Ponyugo *masks during a funeral rite in Tyongofolokaba (near Sinématyali)*

The *Ponyugo* or helmet-masks, carved from a single block of wood, represent several types of animals that symbolize the *Poro* initiation. Although they are often difficult to identify, one of them is fairly characteristic – the *Gbeli-genugo*, also known as *Ghon*, because of its long, flat horns. It appears to the candidates of the first age group at the very beginning of their initiation, and plays a part at the burial of initiates, driving the soul of the deceased once and for all to the land of the dead, as they tend to haunt the place where they have lived. To this end, the mask beats a fast tattoo on a little drum, while stepping over the corpse. Then he proceeds through all the village alleyways, waving a magic horn, the symbol of the power conferred on him by his role in the initiatory institution of the *Poro*.

*Dance of the young girls, at the end of their initiation in Bundyali*

The Senufo practise initiation for girls alongside the men's *Poro*, but in a much more summary fashion that is in no way comparable to the complex rites of the *Poro*. The girls' initiation begins with the operation of excision, and consists of learning the basic principles that every adult woman must know in order to assume her role as wife and mother. However, it is possible for them to acquire a higher initiatory knowledge by entering the *Sandogoso* society, which trains soothsayers and plays an important part in village life.

The arrival of the new initiates is the occasion in certain villages for ceremonial dances (*Kafo*) in which the girls perform in elaborate costumes, wearing helmets and long chains made of cowries.

Nowadays, the girls' *Kafo* dance, known as *Ngoro*, has developed into a folk form. Troups of dancers and musicians have even been set up in several villages in the south of the Bundyali region (Gbato-Senufo country), and come to perform regularly for tourists visiting the area.

# The Malinke

## Ivory Coast (Odyenné region)

Manikomori *rite*

The ancient traditions of the Malinke, also called Manding (Mandingoes), had, before their complete conversion to Islam, many features in common with other peoples of Mande origin, the Bambara (Baumana), the Senufo or Yakuba, for example. The *Manikomori* introduces masked characters whose aim is to mock the excesses of certain members of the community – under the aegis of the judge-mask, the counterpart of the Bambara *Komo* – wearing a costume decorated with feathers, an impressive hood and a wooden trumpet. The other character in this form of social theatre is the monkey-mask, who acts as the 'buffoon', ridiculing the foibles of his contemporaries.

# The Dyula

## Ivory Coast

*Young girl playing the* shantu

The *shantu* is an idiophone made out of a long gourd, open at both ends and sometimes decorated with cowries, as in this photograph. The sound is produced by striking the narrow end with the palm of the hand, giving a sort of muffled hum, and at the same time shaking the instrument like a rattle. This type of instrument, also called a 'thigh-slapper', is found as far away as Nigeria, mainly among the Hausa, whence the term *shantu* originates.

# The Somba  (*pages 94–95*)

## Bénin (Naititingu region)

*Dances of age groups as part of an agrarian ritual*

The Somba do not constitute a very homogenous group, but can be recognized by the way they are organized socially with links to the land. This organization is known as *kubwoti*.

The Somba maintain a system of a fairly large number of age groups (called *kotobe* and *yage*), which naturally only involve men. The whole *kubwoti* brings the different age groups together on the occasions of ritual activities such as rites of passage, ancestor worship and agrarian ceremonies.

In the case of the agrarian rites, the age groups appear only when the first fruits of the millet crop are offered up.

*Leuru Benleng* rite performed by the Fali of Bossum (Cameroon)

Among most of the groups in North Cameroon who have resisted Islam, and whom their Muslim neighbours refer to collectively as *Kirdi*, ancestor worship includes, first and foremost, the cult of the founding ancestor and his direct descendants. The most recent representative is considered 'chief of the earth' or 'chief of the mountain', etc. There is a clear link between this cult and the agrarian rites, and every year offerings are made simultaneously to the ances-

tors and the earth which they control. The Fali call this rite *Leuru Benleng*. The women then come to offer up millet porridge on the consecrated stones. In these photographs, taken more than thirty years ago, the women still wear the traditional G-string, consisting of a belt with a strip of woven fibres falling in a fringe in front. They wear rings of bamboo or twisted lianas on their legs, and clink these together as they dance.

# The Kapsiki

## Cameroon (Mandara region)

*Funeral rites*

The Kapsiki mountain dwellers of northwestern Cameroon inhabit a lunar landscape of bare plateaus dotted with strange peaks. The villages, battered by the sun, whose round huts with pointed thatched roofs blend into the scenery, come to life at the time of seasonal ceremonies or funerals. The funerals exceed the scope of a simple family occasion. Thus, after the lamentations of the close relatives, the deceased, wrapped in strips of cloth, with a thick turban on his head, is carried away on the shoulders of a member of the blacksmiths' caste. The latter are always responsible for burials. According to tradition, the dead man has to be danced along in this way on the blacksmith's shoulders, as if to gladden his spirit at leaving the world of the living. During this rite, the men blow uninterruptedly into flutes bent into the shape of a pipe, while the women, perched on top of the granaries, provide the rhythm by striking their calabashes with the chains and rings that previously served as their G-strings.

# The Matakam

## Cameroon (Oujila region)

In the past, the women used to perform these dances after the harvest at the beginning of the dry season; they were generally intended to pay homage to the earth and the ancestors, as well as to all the women who had tended the fields, from the time of the sowing until the harvest. The pruning hooks carried by the women as they dance stand for renewed fertility and future abundant crops, as emphasized by the crackle of the baskets full of seeds the women wear attached to their legs. These photographs also bear witness to the changes that have occurred in these mountain regions which are the refuge of a number of peoples whom the Fulbe of the plains call *Kirdi*, that is, 'pagans'. Above, photographs taken in the 1950s; on the left, twenty years later.

# The Mousseye

## Chad (Gunu Gaya)

*Possession dance*

The Mousseye, also known as Banana Hoho, inhabit the Central Logone region of Chad, where they concentrate in large numbers around Gunu Gaya. They are excellent farmers and cotton planters, whose traditions link them to their Massa neighbours. Their language is practically identical and they practise a very similar system of divination. Finally, as with the Massa, an 'earth chief' is responsible for the sacrifices and for communicating with the superior powers to ensure the success of the village community's activities. A number of propitiatory rites play a part in agricultural matters, as well as in preparations for collective hunting and fishing expeditions. Among the Mousseye, the phenomenon of possession is extremely important in their religious and social life. The possessed belong to the *fulina* association where they learn the techniques enabling them to become possessed by the spirits. On the occasion of a rain-making ceremony, one of the priests of the *fulina* association carries a hen intended for the sacrifice on his head and beats on a calabash. At the same time, other members of the association blow horns, also made out of gourds, with holes sealed by a membrane in the tubes, which vibrate like fixed reeds. This type of instrument, called a *hoho*, is very characteristic of the Mousseye area, and the word is sometimes used onomatopoeically to refer to the tribe. The ornaments, bead necklaces, belts laden with bells, headdresses, etc., indicate the various categories of spirits whose favours are being sought.

# The Sara

## Chad

*Mating dance of young Sara people from Maro*

**B**oys and girls face each other and perform stamping dances to show off their temperament or physical beauty. Note the abdominal scarring of the girl on the right. This type of relief scarification is obtained by rubbing ash into the cutaneous incisions. These scarifications used to serve a ritual, aesthetic, even erotic, purpose.

The Sara inhabit the extreme southwestern region of Chad in the most fertile part of the country still known as Central Chari, which is, moreover, the most densely populated. They rafter their lands (leaving a place between the furrows) on which they grow abundant crops of millet, sorgho and rice. Among the Sara, the boys' initiation, called *Yondo*, consists of radically transforming the child, the *koy*, the non-initiate, by removing him from all maternal influence, and by the rite of a symbolic death and a sort of alliance with the earth, which causes him to be reborn as a complete man. The initiation includes tests of endurance and courage and the teaching of the basic symbols of the traditional society through the use of a secret language. Towards the end of the initiatory stage, which can last several weeks (formerly several years), the initiates return to the village wearing masks made of leaves. Girls also undergo initiation, the *Ndo Banyan*, which lasts for a shorter period than the boys' *Yondo.*

# The Dangaleat (Hajjeray)

## Chad (Korbo village)

*Dances for the* margay *jinn*

The group commonly called Hajjeray by the Arabs consists of many different peoples who took refuge in the mountainous region of Guera, fleeing from Waddai and Baguirmi incursions. However, they have certain common cultural features, for example, their attachment to the mountains which shelter them, and their worship of the *margay* jinn. In the mountain villages, like the one shown here, the Dangaleat from Korbo organize different ceremonies in honour of these jinn, who represent, in fact, tutelary spirits responsible for controlling the rains and ensuring a

successful harvest. As elsewhere in Subsaharan Africa, these divinities have a double aspect, both good and evil. They manifest themselves by 'possessing' men and women in different ways. Women are 'possessed' in the course of a sometimes spectacular trance, or, in most cases, they are induced 'to dance the *margay*'; for men, on the other hand, the painful presence of the divinities takes the form of illness. Writers have naturally not failed to point out the ambiguity of the *margay*, who can act for man's good by favouring good harvests and, at the same time, manifest themselves by inflicting harm. In reality the misfortunes

that are attributed to them consist of signs that the soothsayer, the specialist of *Gara*, knows how to interpret. What is more, if these divinities were only thought of as harmful, it is unlikely that the Hajjeray or Dangaleat would thank them when the crops are abundant by organizing dances of rejoicing in their honour.

CHAPTER THREE

# Atlantic Coast and Western Wooded Savanna

The Atlantic littoral presents many different features all along the coast, which stretches from Cape Verde to the Bight of Biafra. It is difficult to approach: mangrove swamps, lagoons, reefs, and particularly the bar with its terrible rollers that form near the shore make anchorage dangerous outside a few natural harbours. Nevertheless, from the eleventh to the sixteenth centuries, this coast was the scene of the odious traffic of the slave trade. From the Island of Gorée, from the ports of Ouidah, Benin, Biafra, as far as the mouth of the Wouri, indeed, from even farther south, millions of Africans were forcibly shipped to America to work under the worst possible conditions – in the cane fields, the cotton and tobacco plantations or the mines – often being treated worse than cattle. From this region also came one of the most widespread religions in Subsaharan Africa, that of the Vaudoux system of worship, which gave rise to the Voodoo of Haiti, the Candomblé of Brazil and the Santeria of Cuba. This religion is still practised by the Fon of Benin and the Ewe of Togo, as well as by the Yoruba of Nigeria, whence it originated. Rice-growers and fishermen, like the Baga, the Nalu, and the Diola of Lower Casamance in Senegal, are among the best farmers in the littoral. By working uninterruptedly, they have reclaimed the flooded lands along the whole length of the River Casamance and transformed them into paddy fields. Farther into the interior, the zone is covered by the remains of the former Guinean forest, which has given way to secondary formations or palm groves, according to the altitude. The relatively humid climate is well suited to the cultivation of yams, a tuber that is not only a foodstuff, but also has an important ritual function. It is even possible to speak of a yam civilization, as its growth requires great care and know-how, and as the rites of the first fruit of the yam, which are still practised, mark the renewal of the traditional year for some groups, such as the Ashanti in Ghana, the Yoruba and other neighbouring peoples.

*Huge, two-lipped drum* (ebombolon *or 'talking-drum') made from a solid piece of wood, used by the Diola of Lower Casamance for transmitting messages (Senegal)*

# The Diola

## Senegal (Diembering, Casamance)

*Traditional wrestling rite*

The Diola of Lower Casamance are excellent rice-growers, having invented a most efficient system of polders (reclaimed land that is protected by means of dykes). Their young people's wrestling matches (the *katag* or *kamengen*) are not only a very popular sport, but also a most important moment in the life of the whole village. Every year during the dry season, teams of adolescents from different villages challenge each other to wrestling matches to prove their strength and courage, in short, the vigour of the entire village society. The match is also an opportunity to attract the attention of the girls and possibly find a future wife. After marriage, the young Diola men proceed to a new

*Traditional musical instruments of the Diola of Lower Casamance*

age group and can no longer take part in the traditional wrestling matches. The wrestling itself simply consists of bringing one's adversary to the ground, but the performance entails a long prelude with singing, dancing and provocative parades, during which the last year's champions are carried in triumph and feverishly acclaimed by the audience. It is an honour for a woman to see a champion trample on the scarf or piece of material that she has dropped in front of him. It is customary for the wrestlers to wear fringed belts made from vegetable fibres, similar wrist bands, iron or copper bracelets and the typical leggings made from palmyra fibres. With feathers stuck in their headdress (if possible, those from the sea eagle), they celebrate their victory by dancing and brandishing genuine or symbolic weapons.

In addition to the big two-lipped wooden drums of the *ebombolon* type (also called *kabisa* in some regions), the Diola of Casamance have a variety of drums made of membranes stretched by pegs over a cylindrical or bell-shaped frame (the latter resembling a mortar). Before using the drum, it is advisable to increase the tension of the skin by exposing it to the heat of the fire. The Diola then strike the skin membranes of their drums with their hand or with a stick.

Another of the Diola's typical instruments is the guitar known as the *ekontin* (page 112). It is made from a calabash covered in skin; the neck is a long piece of bamboo, and it generally has three strings. It is used to accompany songs, particularly the songs of praise in honour of the champions in the traditional wrestling matches.

# The Nalu

## Guinea
## (Kukuba Island)

*Dance of the*
Banda *mask*

The Nalu, who came to seek refuge here from the Southern Guinean Coast, have many practices in common with the surrounding peoples, the Baga and Landuman, with whom they are often confused. They also resemble the Diola of Lower Casamance, at least in the way they cultivate the flooded lands that they reclaim from the mangrove swamps. They have, however, a mask which is quite unique, the *Banda*, carved from a single piece of wood. It has a human face with a long jagged jaw, like that of a crocodile, an antelope's horns and, in the centre, a sort of annulated tail representing a snake or a stylized chameleon. In its way, it epitomizes the Nalu's concept of the universe that sur- rounds them, symbolizing three different worlds: that of the bush or the forest, represented by the antelope and the chameleon; that of the water, represented by the crocodile and snake; and, finally, that of the village, represented by a human face. The *Banda* mask used to be very much feared, and women and non-initiates were forbidden to cast eyes on it. It was then the expression of the ritual *Simo* society and represented one of the group's highest grades. It must be pointed out that the mask is extremely heavy and the wearer must dance in such a way as to be able to see in all directions, while whirling round very fast.

# The Kono

Between Guinea, the Ivory Coast and Liberia live several peoples of Mande origin who have great cultural similarities, such as the Kono or Konor, the Dan or Yakuba, the Manu and the Kpelle, or Guerzé. Such similarities are also found among other neighbouring groups, like the Guéré and Wobé (Wè), who speak a different language, however. Their greatest common trait is, in fact, their widespread use of masks, for which there are a great variety of shapes and functions.

Contrary to some popular beliefs, these masks are not necessarily attached to initiation (of the *Poro* type) but appear for all kinds of ritual activities, for example, to commemorate the society's origins, to transmit the myths and history of the village community and its clans or subdivisions or to ensure its peace and safety, etc.

Among the Kono of the Vépo canton, various types of masks can be found, each having its own particular function.

Among the chief masks, the *Nyon nea* or *Nyomu nea*, the female mask with the finely carved face dyed black, and a tall conical headdress, must be mentioned (page 121). This mask represents the 'mother' of the newly circumcised boys, who has 'swallowed' them and caused them to be reborn in the course of the initiation. The *Nyon nea* mask does a dance that is accompanied by horns and drums, and it usually performs together with two other masks of a male type: either the black-faced *Nyon hine*, which is surmounted by a tall cylindrical headdress, or the *Nyon hine gbloa*, a similar mask whose face is covered by a piece of red material. The *Nyon hine gbloa* personifies the 'father' of all the masks and, for this reason, rarely appears.

Another important mask is the *Nyon kpman* or *Nyomu kpman hine*, the red male mask, whose name indicates that it belongs to a warlord (page 120). The Kono masks appear alone or in groups, generally on the occasion of the ceremony following the rice harvest.

*Preceding pages: dance of the principal Kono masks, performed in the middle of the village of Nzo (Guinea) at the harvest festival*

# The Dan (Yakuba)

## Ivory Coast (Man region)

*Gle gben* masks on stilts

This type of mask on stilts has become extremely popular in the so-called three-frontier region: among the Kono, who call it *Nyon* or *Nyomo Kwuya*, and from whom it seems to have originated; among the Dan or Yakuba of the Ivory Coast; as well as among the Toma of Upper Guinea. Normally the mask is worn by a young man capable of executing the most daring acrobatics. These acts are so daring, in fact, that the dance has rapidly become secularized and the mask now appears on all occasions, and its owner tours throughout all the villages of the region, rather like the professional juggler. However, the mask's costume has remained the same as before, give or take a few details. The dancer still hides his face under a net hood, which is dyed black and surmounted by a tall conical headdress decorated with feathers and cowries. He wears long trousers, preferably made out of a striped material, which also cover the whole length of the stilts. The latter, made of palm wood, are fixed to the legs below the knees. The costume is completed by a long-sleeved shirt made of local material, and a short straw or raffia skirt. Nearly three metres tall, the mask performs by twisting and gesticulating, while emitting shrill screeches, to the great delight of the spectators. To demonstrate his acrobatic skill, the mask performs the most dangerous feats – turning upside down, balancing on the roofs of the huts, etc. His manoeuvres are accompanied by one or more vase-shaped drums and by the sound of the bells on the dancer's belt. Mainly a source of entertainment, the *Gle gben* or *Nyon Kwuya* nevertheless belongs to the family of masks and must conform to the rules that apply to them, particularly with regard to the secrets surrounding them, which must never, under any circumstances, be divulged to women or non-initiates.

## The Simbo *acrobatic dances*

Among the Guéré (Wè), there are several groups of dances that are performed solely for pleasure, such as the *Zua* dance in which the dancer seems to be engaged in a kind of rhythmic contest with the musicians.

The *Simbo* or *Sannyulu* acrobatic dances are as popular as the feats performed by the stilt mask, and their fame transcends the western Ivory Coast area. Among the Yakuba and Guéré (Wè), in the Man and Dukoué-Bangolo regions, groups of young athletes and girls regularly perform these dances in the towns and villages.

The origin of the *Simbo* can be traced to ancient traditions linked to methods of immunizing oneself against snake bites.

*The handkerchief dancer*

Simbo *acrobatic dances*

At one time, specialists demonstrated the efficacy of the plants they used by handling extremely poisonous snakes with impunity. Later these demonstrations were replaced by dances in which remarkably supple children writhe and coil like snakes. They are generally little girls, known for this reason as *sannyulu,* who are the best contortionists.

The most spectacular moment in this dance is when the men, known as *simbo,* juggle with the girls, whose faces are painted like those of the initiates, and give the impression of catching them on the tip of a knife, while other little *sannyulu* crawl round their legs, as a reminder of the real origin of these dances.

# FON

## Bénin

*Sacrifice to the* Sakpata voodoo *in Abomey*

*Procession of initiates of the* Hèbioso voodoo *near Cotonou*

The *voodoo* represent spiritual beings, life forces so to speak, and include the divinities to whom the cosmogonic myths attribute the fundamental principles of creation and life on earth. However, every human being eventually becomes a *voodoo* in his turn when he reaches the stage of ancestor. The *voodoo* can be beneficial or harmful, depending on the people and their form of worship. Actually it is through sacrifices that a sort of alliance and mutual assistance are established. The blood of the animals sacrified, considered here as a source of vital energy, is ritually transmitted to the divinities and revives their energy, channelling it for the greatest good of human beings. The animals are sacrificed by the priests and placed on a carpet of consecrated leaves to be watched over by young initiates,

who keep the flies away while waiting for the reincarnated *voodoo* to come to get them.

Before the end of their initiatory training, the new initiates, known as *kwèdanu*, participate in different rites that aim at preparing them to receive the *voodoo* and to act as its representative in its many manifestations. That is why the new initiates always have shaved heads and bare shoulders: it is a sign of respect for the *voodoo*, which is called upon to 'descend on their head'. Children are frequently initiated at the same time as their mothers and accompany them during the whole period of initiation.

Gbehun *dance of the* Sakpata voodoo *in Abomey*

**S**akpata (called *Shopona* by the Yoruba) is the name given to the many different appearances and manifestations of the *voodoo* on earth. One of the most popular with the Fon, *Sakpata*, is also known as the smallpox *voodoo*, as it has the ability to make all sorts of seeds germinate – not only those that grow in the earth but also the pustules on its victims' skin.

After sacrifices have been made to them, the *Sakpata voodoo* are reincarnated through the initiates, who are dressed in multicoloured costumes: typically the short, hooped skirts, known as *vlaya*, which they whirl round as they perform the rapid *gbehun* dance, whose name perfectly expresses the vitality and nature of this *voodoo*. One of them wields a *récade*, an angled wooden sceptre or staff of office, decorated with silver appliqués, which, in the period of the Abomey Kingdom, was the insignia of a royal messenger.

# The Yoruba

## Bénin (Cové region)

### Gelede *masks*

Originally, the *Gelede's* purpose was to combat sorcery (the many magico-religious practices that endanger the social equilibrium and traditional customs) and, in so doing, was associated with *Efe*, another of the masks' institutions. But, whereas *Efe* appears especially at night, the *Gelede* only performs during the day. Many authors on the subject claim that the *Gelede* issues from the power of the 'mothers'. Indeed, the Yoruba expression for sorcery, *aje*, is a contraction of *iyaje*, whose literal meaning is 'mother-food'. In general, pronouncing this word is avoided, so as not to attract the attention of actual or potential sorcerers, those known as *aje*, who have the ability to change into birds at night.

These dances are interspersed with burlesque interludes performed by animal masks that represent well-known characters from the oral literature, popular tales or moral fables. Here, for example, the *Ayoko* mask, perched on stilts, amuses the spectators at the expense of the hyena, the animal thought to be the most treacherous and stupid of all the creatures in the bush.

The two female masks represent twins. The Yoruba, like some of their neighbours, hold twins in great esteem, and their presence in a family is a sign of good fortune and happiness. In addition to the head mask with the elaborate plaited coiffure, the two dancers are rigged out with false wooden breasts, and wear jangling anklets called *iku*.

In many cases, behaviour that deviates from accepted norms, the result of certain innovations, is thought to be a factor for disorder, the source of conflict and tension that encourages recourse to all kinds of magic practices – in a word, sorcery.

With a view to averting these disasters, the *Gelede* enables the traditional conscience to be revived, mobilizes it, so to speak, to protect the social order that is threatened by neglect and by apparently harmful new customs. Using these masks, the *Gelede* first tries to obtain the goodwill of the 'mothers' or occult powers through a flattering and colourful ritual, while at the same time affirming the social and cultural traditions, and deriding those who attempt to

upset them. Nowadays the institution mainly retains the character of a social satire and the appearance of popular theatre.

The *Gelede* generally appear in pairs – male and female (*Akogi* and *Abogi*). The dancers are hidden under loose cotton tunics, wear a wooden mask set on top of their head and sometimes have wooden props fixed to their bellies or their backs.

The ideal image of the mother is expressed here by a female mask, with the addition of a statuettte or 'body mask' representing a child at the breast.

# CHAPTER FOUR

# Central
# and
# East Africa

Central Africa, our last stage on the African journey that is the purpose of this book, consists, first and foremost, of all the peoples who are related to the huge Bantu family of languages. This does not mean that they belong to a single cultural stock, although they may possess certain common characteristics: the system of chiefdoms and the secret societies, such as those of the Bamileke in Cameroon, for example; or the part played by the *Nyanga*, both sorcerer and healer. This great African equatorial forest region is also a sort of mythical Africa, as suggested by the picture of the Mbuti pygmies addressing the spirits of the deepest forest in the valley of the Ituri in Zaire, where they are to be found. Mythical, too, are the displays that are reminders of the power of the former Kuba kings: the subtle body decorations of the women of the ancient Mangbetu Kingdom (noted by the German traveller Georg August Schweinfurth in 1870) and the dances of the former Tutsi warriors of Rwanda, which became a part of folklore in the colonial period. Both the geography and history of East Africa are different from the rest of the continent. In fact, to the east of the deep fault known as the Rift Valley, which stretches from Zimbabwe to the foot of the Ethiopian Massif, is an immense grassy plain that is chiefly travelled by Masai cattle-breeders. These volcanic lands, at heights of between three thousand and over six thousand feet, seem to favour human settlement, even though the problem of water remains unsolved. The rift is thought to have had other more important results for the history of mankind. Some, led by Professor Y. Coppens, claim that, as it rose, the eastern part of Africa grew drier, and the humid tropical forest gave way to steppe and to sparse vegetation. These conditions would have determined the appearance of our first human ancestors, the australopithecines, more than two million years ago.

*Procession of the Bamum sultan's heralds, in Fumban, with their long* kakaki *horns,*
*which are similar to those of the Lamido Fulbe from North Cameroon*

# The Bamum

## Cameroon (Fumban)

The Bamum, descended, as they themselves declare, from the Tikar people, founded a powerful kingdom in the hilly plateau area known as Grassfield in western Cameroon. They supplanted the many petty chiefdoms of the previous inhabitants, of Bamileke or Tikar origin, who did not form a coherent ensemble capable of repelling the invaders. The Bamum kingdom reached the height of its power during the nineteenth century, in the reign of King Mbuömbuö, a legendary figure whose warlike exploits still pervade the repertoire of the *griots*, or storytellers. It was he who succeeded in extending the frontiers of the kingdom as far as the Mbam and the Nun, the two main rivers that mark the southern and western boundaries of the present-day Department of Bamum.

The Bamum have many features in common with their Tikar and Bamileke neighbours, as much from the point of view of language as from that of culture in general; they share the same concept of the world and of the supernatural forces that govern it, of the role of the ancestors, chiefdoms and secret societies.

*Members of the* Mütngu *secret society*

The members of this society formed the king's police force and were responsible for carrying out the royal decrees. Their supreme chief was the *Tangu* or 'father of the country' who occupied an exceptional rank among the notables of the kingdom, as it was his duty to see that the customs were respected, even by the king. The members of the *Mütngu* were recruited from among the palace servants.

*War dance of the* Mbansie

Armed with spears, their faces smeared with soot or blue powder, the members of the *Mbansie* society extol in their songs and dances the Bamum's traditional deeds of valour, in particular the exploits of the celebrated King Mbuömbuö. They wear characteristic headdresses, the insignia of their rank, and little leather or woven bags containing a number of amulets or magic objects; they also carry the wide, short-bladed cutlass in its typical wooden case with two handles.

*Masks formerly worn by the secret societies*

At the time of the kingdom every secret society based in the palace had its own musical instruments, insignias and masks. So, for example, the *Nsoro* society had black masks with protruding eyes that were worn on top of the head as reminders of the exploits of the members of this warlike society. The masks photographed here, 'in action', date from the time of King Njoya, but are no longer worn: they now belong to the collection in the Museum of the Bamum Arts and Traditions in Fumban.

The former Bamum sultan, El Hadj Seidou Njimoluh Njoya, is pictured (third from the right, above) with his retinue and, in the foreground, a musician playing the *Müjömndü* double bell, one of the symbols of Bamum royalty.

# The Bamileke

## Cameroon (Banjun and Baleng region)

The term 'Bamileke' covers a collection of peoples from the Upper Mbam who sought refuge – following the Tikar, Bamum and Fulbe invasions – in the highlands and valleys of West Cameroon, where they inhabit one of the most densely populated areas of Subsaharan Africa. An industrious people, the Bamileke have turned their region into fertile farmlands, making use of the smallest corner of earth for their subsistence crops, their cola and coffee plantations, or for growing the long bamboo which they formerly used to construct their huts. Traditionally their social life is organized around the person of the chief, who lives in what is called the chieftainry, a fairly important collection of huts intended for habitation or ritual activities. That is where the chief's wives and descendants live, as well as a number of servants, who are the officials responsible for transmitting the chief's orders and seeing that they are carried out. There are also, in every chieftainry, several secret societies, each one having a definite role, that is either political, like the Kamvö, or religious, like the Kungang.

*Members of secret societies in ceremonial garb*

On the occasion of seasonal celebrations, or for the funeral of one of their members, as well as for the enthronement of the chief, the secret societies perform in public, in processions and dances, showing off their costumes and insignia of office. Above: a representative of the Kamvö, with his long blue cloak, accompanied by a member of the *Kuintang* society (in charge of justice) in his mantle of leaves. At right: members of the chief's *Manjong*, who are responsible for local policing.

142

Tso *dance of the Kuosi society*

One of the most spectacular dances is undoubtedly the *Tso*, which demonstrates all of the prestige and vigour of the chiefdom. It is performed by members of the traditionally warlike *Kuosi* society who wear richly beaded fabric hoods, with ears and a long flap hanging down in front, that are reminiscent of elephants; hence the name 'elephant-mask' given it by Europeans. The dancers are dressed in a tie-dyed indigo fabric trimmed with red braid, waistcoats completely covered with bead embroidery, headdresses of feathers or fabric, and leopard skins, a sign of their rank in society. The dances obtain their rhythm from drums (in particular, the bowl-shaped *nkak*), xylophones (simply made from pieces of wood placed on two palm trunks) and from iron bells and rattles similar to maracas (made from wickerwork and filled with seeds).

# The Banda

## Central African Republic
## (Bangui region)

*Gaza dance of young female initiates*

The aim of the initiation, here termed the *Gaza*, is to transform young people into adults capable of assuming their roles in traditional society. For the girls initiation consists, first and foremost, of their becoming child-bearing women, able to fulfil their function as wives.

At the end of their initiatory retreat, the young people express through their dances their joy at having succeeded in triumphing over the ordeals of this rite of passage. On this occasion the girls wear loincloths or short skirts made from shredded fibres and beaded sashes and necklaces (symbols of their femininity), and they perform (alone or in groups) very expressive, and usually extremely graceful, dances to the sound of the drums.

# The Kuyu

Congo

*Figures from of the* Kyebe-Kyebe *dance*

**F**ormerly, on the occasion of initiation to the *Djo* cult (worship of the mythical serpent), the Kuyu called on masked figures, the *Ehuya*, who danced holding up carved wooden puppets over their heads. The aim of the performance, reserved solely for initiates, was to retrace the great moments of the Kuyu society's mythical history. Since then, the *Ehuya* 'masks' have taken on a much more secular character in the form of the *Kyebe-Kyebe* dances, which nowadays take place in public, their sole aim being entertainment. The dancers are hidden under huge cotton or hessian garments from which the plumed puppets stick out. The dances, accompanied by drums, whistles or bells and the spectator's chanting, provide a very popular display. They involve veritable exercises in virtuosity, in the course of which the actors execute very rapid, elegant pirouettes, lifting their puppets up very high in the air, then dropping them down to the ground to form, if possible, a perfect cone.

# The Njabi

Gabon (M'Bigou region)

Mukuyi *white mask on stilts*

**T**he white masks of southern Gabon were, for a long time, wrongly attributed to the Mpongwe from the mouth of the River Ogué, and to the coastal Lumbo, who, in fact, merely sold them to the Europeans.

The white masks of the Eshira, Punu, Sango and Njabi peoples, called *Mukuyi* or *Mukudji*, are used in the commemorative celebrations for the ancestors or in funeral rites better known by the name *Bwitii*. The white colour of the face is, in fact, a reminder of the deceased, specifically a women returning from the realm of the dead. The feminine character of the mask is emphasized by the very elaborate coiffure in the shape of a coconut shell with plaited hair hanging from each side, and by the graceful, delicate facial features. In addition, the use of stilts confers an unusual, one may even say superhuman, dimension on the masks. It should be noted in passing that other white masks are to be found elsewhere in Subsaharan Africa where they have more or less the same role, as does, for example, the *Mmaw* masks of the Ibo in Nigeria.

# The Teke

## Congo (Gamboma)

*Dance of the* Mfumu *chiefs*

The Teke or Tyo, as they call themselves, form one of the most important ethnic groups of the present Congo Republic (formerly French Congo, or Congo-Brazzaville). Long before the Portuguese arrived at the mouth of the river, the Teke's ancestors founded a powerful kingdom far surpassing that of the Kongo and Loango. The Teke kingdom took an active part in the slave trade, through the intermediary of the Loango, and reached the height of its power between the seventeenth and eighteenth centuries, invading the Kongo territories on the other side of the river. The social organization of the Teke and neighbouring groups of peoples, such as the Lari, Sundi and Bwembe, rests traditionally on the hierarchical distribution of power among the chiefs of the clans and the village or on regional chiefs, all of whom are placed under the authority of the king, the *makoko*. The latter, who is both spiritual and political chief, is elected by the elders of the kingdom from one of the six clans or branches of the royal family.

As elsewhere in Subsaharan Africa, the power of the chiefs is surrounded by a sacred aura that is reinforced by the possession of magic or highly symbolic objects. This mysterious power is also indicated by their garments, adornments and accessories; for example, the headdress decorated with the feathers of birds, often of those with a specific significance, or the facial painting in colours that may signify some aspect of the chief's character. Thus, eyes outlined in white clay (*pembe*) prove that the chief is capable of seeing into the next world, or that he holds the secrets of the future – is he not, in fact, the interpreter of the will of the ancestors? Other elements of the chief's attire also have a symbolic value: the necklace of leopard's teeth confers the strength or other characteristics of this beast as they appear in the oral traditions; similarly, the cap, decorated with a double row of cowries in front, represents the seat of superior forces. Mention must also be made of the various accessories that are inseparable from the chief's ceremonial garb, such as fly-whisks, knives or ritual copper axes, etc.

*Dance of the* Ebanigi, *as performed by the Teke of Ewo (Congo Republic)*

The *Ebanigi*'s dance expresses the former warlike traditions of the Teke kingdom, of which they were once the military elite in the service of the king, the *Makoko*. In the course of this dance, the *Ebanigi* prove their bellicose nature by brandishing all sorts of weapons, including cutlasses and a number of strangely shaped throwing knives. They smear their bodies and faces with white clay, *pembe*, and carry huge bunches of multicoloured feathers.

# The Kuba (Bushong)

## Zaire (Mushenge region)

*Inauguration of the* Moshambwooy *royal mask*

The Kuba ethnic group consists of several peoples of whom the Bushong, who founded a flourishing kingdom between the Kasai and Sankuru Rivers, predominate. The traditions of this illustrious past, handed down by an abundant oral literature, are maintained to the present day by the Bushong, who still have a profound respect for their king, the *nyim*. In fact, they still consider him the representative of *Woot*, the legendary king, son of *Mbwoom*, who begat all the Kuba. That is why they give him the title of King of the Bushong and god of the earth.

This greatness and nobility of the Kuba kings is particularly conveyed in a very elaborate court etiquette, in a royal art that has produced many masterpieces (principally in the form of wooden carvings such as effigies of former kings), and in their sumptuous costumes.

Among the masks, the *Moshambwooy* or *Mwaashambwooy* plays a very important part in the ritual of royalty, as it possesses a mystical reality with which the king is identified. The royal mask, in the form of a helmet with the face covered by leopard skin and decorated with beads and cowries, has a characteristic crest made of eagle's feathers, the *ibeky*. It is worn by the king for solemn ceremonies, or by the *Muyum*, who is his spiritual double. It is also the funeral mask of important chiefs: those who achieved the privilege of wearing eagles' feathers in their headdresses.

The *Moshambwooy* has the richest costume of all the royal dances: it consists of several parts that completely cover the dancer's body and are all embroidered with beads and cowries. The dancers to whom the king lends the royal masks must perform the long ceremonial inauguration of the masks, each of which receives its own name. The dance of the *Moshambwooy* consists of a sequence of complex figures all performed with great dignity.

# The Salampasu

## Zaire (The Luiza region)

*Masks of the* Mfuku *dance*

The Salampasu, whose name means 'men with the locust tattoos', settled between the tributaries of the Kasai and Lulua rivers, with the greatest density on the west bank of the latter. Hunters, like the Tshokwe, the Salampasu have gained a solid reputation as fierce warriors renowned for cutting off the heads of their enemies. This reputation was certainly fostered, indeed enhanced, by the erstwhile societies or brotherhoods that united all the warriors and practised rites and dances with the aim of firing their courage or warlike ardour. At the same time, they were also concerned with impeding any possible posthumous vengeance on the part of their victims. These societies consisted of different grades and performed masked dances, such as the *mfuku*. The initiation rites and dances, reserved exclusively for men, are the occasion for the appearance of various types of masks worn by the masters of the brotherhoods. They nearly always have a bulging forehead and a flat nose, with a headdress of feathers or plaited balls of vegetable fibres. The majority of the masks are made of wood covered with copper, like the *Mulandwa*, but there are others that are made of dyed black netting and have a conical headdress decorated with coloured triangles. The dancers wear waistcoats made of loosely plaited fibres, a shredded bark skirt and leopard skins, and they brandish fearsome-looking swords, antelope horns or bells.

# The Komo (Kumu)

## Zaire (Madula region)

*Nsembu masks and the ritual* nkunda *actors*

The Komo, a forest people dispersed throughout the region to the southeast of Kisangani, have no chiefdoms or traditional political organization; their ethnic conscience depends rather on the spread of certain socio-cultural ideas. It is important to point out that the whole of this region suffered badly at the end of the nineteenth century from Arab raids in search of slaves that resulted in the massacre and uprooting of African peoples. Generally speaking, the Komo form their settlements in sections from the same lineage and rest their social structure mainly on the practice of the *esumba* rites, which are reserved for men. These include, for example, the circumcision rites (and the formation of the age groups), the *mpunzu* initiation rites associated with the former, and, finally, the *nkunda* rites relating to the initiation of soothsayers, the *bafumu* or *abakunda*. The latter actually form an independent association, organized in a hierarchical system, with its own meeting place (the house of the *nkunda*), dances, costumes and various ritual objects, such as statuettes or masks. Although no one can be completely certain, it is thought that the oval-shaped masks, which are generally multicoloured, also form part of the *nkunda* ritual, in which they could represent different types of characters following the progression of the dance. These masks, called *Nsembu*, would appear at the funeral of a member of the soothsayers' association and in the course of the initiation of the *bafumu* or in the solemn divination sessions, but always at night and solely in the presence of the initiates. The *nkunda* dances bring together the new *bafumu* soothsayers who decorate themselves for the occasion, according to their grade and their function, with feathers, leather or bark belts, ivory bracelets and little bells hung from their arm bands.

# The Mbuti

## Zaire (Ituri region)

*Dance sequences, part of the* molimo made *rite*

The Mbuti Pygmies, living as they do, cut off in the depths of the Ituri forests, have been able to pursue their traditional existence as hunter-gatherers. But everywhere else Pygmies have been more or less absorbed by their neighbours of Bantu origin, as in the case of the Southern African Bushmen. The purpose of most of the Mbuti's rites is propitiation, before a hunting expedition for instance, but they also constitute a sort of 'reparation' to the forest and its spirit inhabitants. Thus, every year, the rite known as *molimo made* is performed to wipe out offences commit-

ted by members of the community against the spirits of the woods. This rite is sometimes combined with collective fustigations, which have been compared to a sort of social catharsis. All of these rites are accompanied by dancing to the beat of an enormous drum, and by the chanting of the women whose sophisticated polyphony has inspired the admiration of musicologists. The Mbuti play a sort of harp – also found among other groups inhabiting the region, particularly the Zande and Mangbetu – alongside their chanting.

# The Mangbetu

## Zaire (Nanga region)

*Women in traditional attire*

The Mangbetu, of Sudanese origin like their neighbours the Zande, inhabit savanna land on the edge of the great Uele forest which, before them, had been home to the Pygmies and various other groups of Bantu origin, such as the Lese, the Komo, the Mamvu, etc. The Mangbetu founded a powerful kingdom in this region around the nineteenth century, before being overcome by the Zande. When the German botanist and explorer Schweinfurth found his way into their territory in 1870, the Mangbetu (or Mombouttous as he called them in the French version of his book) were still at the height of their power. He was very impressed by their socio-political organization, their artistic techniques and the many cultural activities at the court of King Munza, and he never tired of singing their praises.

The many masterpieces of the Mangbetu, such as their wooden sculptures, are well known. In the past, they were masters in the crafts of forging fearsome weapons, building large palaces, producing elegant clay models and making good-quality fabric from beaten bark, etc. The Mangbetu's concern for aesthetics, which was the basis of what emerged as a brilliant court art, is even more evident in their costume and body art. Once upon a time their dress was reduced to its simplest expression: a piece of bark tied at the waist for the men and, for the women, a thong or strip of cloth with which they covered themselves to sit down. For certain occasions the women wore an apron of beaten bark dyed dark brown and the typical *negbe*, a sort of buttock-covering, also made of beaten bark and decorated with remarkably elaborate geometric patterns. Both men and women had elongated skulls, produced by compressing the babies' heads in string nets. In addition, the women used to paint their whole bodies in elaborate patterns, using the sap of the gardenia, and they would braid their hair on a wickerwork frame to form tall funnel-shaped cylinders in which they stuck ivory or wooden pins.

# The Alur

## Zaire (Lake Mobutu region)

*Dance of the young initiates*

The Alur, with a population of more than two hundred thousand, live to the west of Lake Mobutu (formerly Lake Albert) and on the banks of the Albert Nile, between Uganda and Zaire. Like their neighbours and close kin the Acholi, they are of Nilotic origin and, in common with them, they grow cereals, mainly sorgho, and naturally also rear cattle. In their religion, the Alur have many things in common with the other Nilotic stock-breeders; for example, they celebrate the possession ritual known as *Jok*, which means spirit in general and mainly takes the form of ancestor worship and therapeutic seances.

The system of age groups, on the other hand, linked to the initiation of children between the ages of ten and twelve, seems much less widespread with the Alur than in the other Nilotic groups. Nevertheless, the Alur share some of their customs, such as the extraction of the lower incisors, and they also organize celebrations at the end of the initiation period, when boys and girls paint white spots on their bodies and perform all kinds of dances. It must not be forgotten that the Alur were for a long time in contact with Bantu groups, mainly the Bantu kingdom of Bunyoro which has left deep traces on the history and beliefs of this people.

# The Tutsi

## Rwanda

*Dance of the* intore

In bygone days, the *intore* (the chosen ones) used to form the warrior elite of the kingdom. In the colonial period their dancing was much appreciated by the Europeans, and they would perform for all important ceremonies. The *intore* dancers, richly bedecked with bead necklaces and wearing their typical headdresses with the long raffia manes, would hurl themselves about and leap impressively, while brandishing bows and spears, to the accompaniment of the *amakondera*, or 'horn players'. Finally, the leading dancer would perform a solo, to the delight of the spectators whom he captivated by the graceful movements of a dance that demonstrated his courage and skill to the full.

*Group of* ingoma *drums*

The group consists of about ten large drums with tied membranes, of different pitch, which are struck with flat sticks. There are several rhythms, always introduced by a solo player and taken up by the group, and each tells its own story.

*Musician playing the* inanga *zithar*

The long *inanga* zithar, with six or seven strings stretched over a hollowed-out board, was used in the past to accompany the *ibisogo* dynastic chants.

# The Masai

## Tanzania (Ngorongoro)

Distributed all along the great Rift Valley, between Kenya and Tanzania, the Masai still cling fiercely to their traditions as nomadic herdsmen. In fact, their herds represent their great pride, and they affect a certain contempt for those among them who have been forced into a sedentary existence and till the soil. Apart from stock-breeding, the Masai have a passion for hunting and cattle-rustling, which gives them the opportunity of satisfying their taste for war and adventure, although present-day conditions do not allow them to indulge in this as much as they would like.

*Recently circumcised boys*

Circumcision, known as *emorata*, is a most important event in the life of a Masai boy as it will determine his entry, his passage, into the warrior class. After the operation, when the wound has sufficiently healed, the newly circumcised boys are fêted by their comrades, who decorate their faces with white paint. They make themselves headdresses out of the feathers of birds, which they are now allowed to hunt, and they wear their mothers' copper ornaments (*isurutia*).

*Dance of the young* Ilmoran *warriors*

The Masai dancers perform impressively high leaps on the spot, their bodies straight upright and draped in cloaks, while the spectators do not spare their shouts of enthusiasm. In these photographs there is no denying their proud bearing, with their long hair braided into little pigtails and stuck through with all kinds of ornaments, their bead necklaces (signs of their success with girls) and their long sticks or clubs, which replace the spears that are now forbidden by the authorities but which are no less formidable weapons in their hands.

# Bibliography

## Works of general interest

Ajahi, J. F. A., and Crowder, Michael, *Historical Atlas of Africa* (London: Longman, 1985).

Alexandre, Pierre, *Les Africains* (Paris: Ed. Lidis, 1981).

Bebey, Francis, *Musique de l'Afrique* (Paris: Horizon de France, 1969).

*Découverte de l'Afrique Noire* (Paris: Larousse, 1968).

*Dictionnaire des Civilisations Africaines* (Paris: P. Hazan, 1968).

Fischer, Angela, *Africa Adorned* (London: Collins, 1984).

Gourou, Pierre, *L'Afrique* (Paris: Hachette, 1970).

Huet, Michel, and Keita, Fodeba, *Les Hommes de la Danse* (Lausanne: Ed. Clairefontaine, 1954).

Huet, Michel; Laude, Jean, and Paudrat, Jean-Louis, *Danses d'Afrique* (Paris: Ed. du Chêne, 1978).

Ki-Zerbo, Joseph, *Histoire de l'Afrique Noire: d'Hier à Demain* (Paris: Hatier, 1972).

Meyer, Laure, *Black Africa: Masks, Sculpture, Jewelry* (Paris: P. Terrail, 1994).

Nketia, K. J. H., *Music of Africa* (New York: W. W. Norton & Co., 1974; London: Gollancz, 1986).

Thomas, Louis-Vincent, and Luneau, René, *La Terre Africaine et ses Religions* (Paris: Larousse, 1975).

———, *Les Religions d'Afrique Noire* (Paris: Fayard, 1969).

UNESCO, *Practical Guide to the World Decade of Cultural Development, 1988–1997* (Paris: UNESCO, 1988).